bored in Paris

Awesome Experiences for the Repeat Visitor

dean dalton
+
andie easton

Cover art created by Dean Dalton

bored in Paris

Introduction

Part I - Try a Group Experience   1
❧View things differently as part of a pack

Part 2 - Connect with Nature   13
❧Outdoor activities in and around Paris

Part 3 - Learn Something New   25
❧And gain knowledge of the culture

Part 4 - Search for Something   37
❧Hunting for Parisian goodies is fun

Part 5 - Have an Engrossing Individual Experience   49
❧Make it all about you

Part 6 - Make Memories   61
❧Share delightful moments with loved ones

Part 7 - Local Thrills and Chills   77
❧Some of Paris's more hair-raising sights

Part 8 - Be a Child Again   89
❧Places and activities to share with your kids

From the Authors
Index

Paris again?

Okay, so you've been to Paris before and are planning another trip there. Great. But what will make this visit special? What will set this trip apart? When you're already familiar with Paris' main sights, this unique travel book will provide inspiration and get your brain humming with fun recommendations that will have you laughing, tasting, and participating in things you may have never considered. This book is literally full of awesome experiences that will open up a whole new side of Paris, a side that millions of tourists still don't know about. You'll be able to immerse yourself just like a true Parisian.

You might be thinking, *But I don't speak French, so how can I do some of these things?* These days, that concern is almost laughable. Ordinary French people now speak English, and the ones who are in charge of special activities and experiences really*, really* speak English. Some of the activities included here have very little verbal communication involved anyway.

Have you always wanted to ride a horse or learn how to make croissants but just never had the time? Do it when you're in Paris, while you're away from the daily grind of your busy life. That's what free time should be about. As you encounter our curated list of incredible things to see and do, you'll find that they vary greatly. Because we can't know every reader personally, we included experiences that range from completely free, to cheapy-cheap, to kind of pricey but totally worth it. Some of these experiences are right in the city center while others are in the countryside but still easy to get to. Many are interactive or hands-on, while others are merely something to see and absorb. Several are for active people and some are for the typical couch potato. That means we've tried our best to include something just for *you*, whoever you are.

While reading through our lists, your own visit to Paris will begin to take shape in your mind. You may even feel some level of excitement. This is why we must remind you that some of our curated activities, classes, and unique sights are more popular than others (or have smaller groups) and will therefore need to be booked in advance. Luckily, almost all are cancelable if your plans should change once you've arrived in Paris.

A quick note about the verbiage and info you'll encounter here: we refer to all the main sights and well-known neighborhoods as if you've been to Paris before. If you're a novice and come across a place or word you've never heard of, go ahead and look it up. We don't mind.

So, whatever kind of traveler you are... no matter if you've already visited the Eiffel Tower a million times or have never been here before, this book will make it impossible to ever be bored in Paris!

Happy travels to all,
Dean & Andie

P.S. No one has ever paid us, coerced us, or even comp'd us to include the places and experiences in this book, (or in any of our books.) Only a few even know that they are mentioned here, and that's the way we like it.

Part 1

Try a Group Experience
❖ View things differently as part of a pack ❖

Group activities are a great way to share in a unique experience while having fun *and* making new friends. Don't be intimidated that you might not be up to the "expectations" of the group; we've found time and time again that both the participants and leaders in these activities always go above and beyond to make sure the less comfortable, or less energetic in the pack, are treated with respect and given every chance to enjoy themselves as well. There's nothing like a shared experience to launch a lasting friendship and the ones we chose for this chapter are fantastic.

"Paris is always a good idea."

Join a Super-Fun Pub Crawl
through the Latin Quarter

Sure, you could go bar hopping in the *Quartier Latin* on your own. Easy, right? The thing is…this isn't like that. This group experience is super-fun because it's organized by the amazing folks at *Riviera Bar Crawls Paris* and that means a night you'll not soon forget. After being introduced to the other guests, their amazing hosts will take you to the most festive bars for drinks and games and then end the night at one of the city's biggest clubs. Free entry is included, as well as a free shot and drink discounts, at every single bar. We don't want to give any of their surprises away so let's just say it's like a moving party and we know you'll have a blast!

rivierabarcrawltours.com/pub-crawl-paris

Located at 25 Rue Frédéric Sauton
In the 5th arrondissement, Paris

Intl. calling: (011) 33 7 69 59 91 62
Local calling: 07 69 59 91 62

Email: paris@rivierabarcrawl.com

Offered most nights, and *every* night in summer
Closed on major holidays

Ages 18 to 80 are welcome!

See a French Film
with English Subtitles

Movie cinemas here regularly show American films, but who wants to see those while you're visiting Paris? The problem is, those wonderful French films are usually presented as "v.o." which indicates *version originale*. That means if the movie was filmed in French then it is being shown the same way. So can visitors find a *French* film with *English* subtitles? You betcha.

Thanks to a unique organization called "Lost in Frenchlation," you can join a group of like-minded film enthusiasts for a cocktail hour, a viewing of a French film with English subtitles, and even some live entertainment to boot. This allows Parisians *and* the international community to mingle and enjoy an evening together, and a screening that won't leave you wondering what the heck the film was about.

lostinfrenchlation.com

The scheduled events of this fantastic organization are held at many different film venues around Paris.

Intl. calling: (011) 33 6 67 33 39 75
Local calling: 06 67 33 39 75

Email: lostinfrenchlation@gmail.com

Their website is everything. Check it for upcoming screenings.

Be Part of an Interactive
Food Crawl in the Marais

The culinary experts at "Paris By Mouth" offer fabulous food crawls in many different neighborhoods but our favorite is the one in the quaint area of the Marais on the Right Bank. These small group, culinary walking tours are designed to let you experience the things that Paris does best, like pastry, bread, charcuterie, chocolate, wine and cheese. During the stroll you'll visit true artisanal shops and sample foods in each. After that you'll spend time seated in a wine shop where the pairing of French wines and cheeses will be the delicious focus. *Formidable!*

parisbymouth.com/food-wine-tours

Meeting place will be disclosed upon booking
In the city center, Paris

Intl. calling: (011) 33 9 70 73 66 99
Local calling: 09 70 73 66 99

Email: tasteparisbymouth@gmail.com

Tours offered daily, by reservation only
Book your spot on their website or by email

Join Parisians in a
Serene Yoga Class

Go and find your bliss. **Paris Yoga Shala** is located just a block away from the main area of the city's top designer boutiques, and not far from the famous Avenue des Champs Elysées. They offer many classes in both English and French where attendees engage in the methods of *Shala Hatha*, *Ashtanga*, *Vinyasa*, *Yin*, and Restorative yoga. All levels and ages are welcome here. You can even book a one-on-one, private session.

parisyoga.com

Located at 9 Rue Magellan
In the 8th arrondissement, Paris

Intl. calling: (011) 33 1 40 70 14 44
Local calling: 01 40 70 14 44

Email: contact@parisyoga.com

Classes held everyday from around 7:30am to 7pm or later
Call to inquire about space & availability

Savor a Pop Up Dinner
in a Chef's Own Flat

For great cuisine and lively conversation, join other food-lovers at a pop up dinner in the city center. Philippe will cook a three course French meal served with aperitifs and wine. You'll meet, and dine with, others from around the world as you enjoy roasted Camembert and other traditional fare, including a surprise dessert. Vegetarian and food sensitivity requests can be honored. Why go to a restaurant when you can have dinner (or lunch) inside a chef's own home?

eatwith.com/events/2843

Located near the Cathedral of Notre Dame
In the 1st arrondissement, Paris

Telephone number and address are given upon your booking with "EatWith"

Email: support@eatwith.com

Check the website calendar for current available dates

Join a Crêpe-Making
Luncheon on the Left Bank

Join a small group of food and dessert devotees from around the world to savor a traditional French quiche and salad lunch with wine, and then receive a hands-on lesson in the making of sweet crêpes. From the special recipe to the correct techniques, you'll have a wonderful learning experience and meet new people at the same time. Kids are welcome too!

eatwith.com/events/22804

Located on the western side of the Left Bank
In the 15th arrondissement, Paris

Calling from the US or Canada: (1) 844-880-5316
Calling from Paris (001) 844-880-5315 (customer service)
Telephone number and address of your host is given upon your booking with "EatWith"

Email: support@eatwith.com

Held daily from 12:30pm to 2:30pm
Check the website calendar for current available dates

Rollerblade at Night with Thousands of Enthusiasts

Now a Paris tradition, organized rollerblading through the streets of Paris takes place every Friday night and Sunday afternoon. If you're a decent skater then you shouldn't miss this. There's even a full police escort *on skates* at both events.

Before choosing which group to join, consider how comfortable you are on those rollerblades. The Friday night group skates for over seventeen miles and has some downhills and cobblestones to look out for. The Sunday group is much more relaxed and has skaters of varying levels, even some families, with the fastest skaters always in the prime position out front.

To officially join either group, sign up online at the website below and show up with your rollerblades thirty minutes beforehand. Skaters who actually join the association will receive free insurance against an accident. The association strongly encourages all participants to wear protective gear such as helmets and wrist guards. So fun and it's free!

rollers-coquillages.org

Rollers & Coquillages - **a relaxed skating event**
Sundays from 2:30pm to 5:30pm (weather permitting)

Meet at Place de la Bastille around 2pm
In the 11th arrondissement, Paris

Intl. calling: (011) 33 1 44 54 94 42
Local calling: 01 44 54 94 42

Email: infos@rollers-coquillages.org

(continued)

pari-roller.com

Friday Night Fever - **the Pari Roller event**
Sundays from 10pm to 1am (weather permitting)

**Meet between Place Raoul Dautry and the
Montparnasse train terminal around 9:30pm**
In the 14th arrondissement, Paris

Intl. calling: (011) 33 1 44 18 30 39
Local calling: 01 44 18 30 39

Email: contact@pari-rollers.com

Explore Monet's Gardens
with a Group Visit to Giverny

The brilliant impressionist artist, Claude Monet took up residence in Giverny, a little town on the Seine about an hour northwest of Paris. His quaint home and spectacular gardens there were a constant inspiration to him. After his passing, the Monet family granted it all to the state for which it has been maintained ever since. Believe us when we say that you have never seen a garden like this one. You will love this tour even if you have no particular interest in flowers or impressionist art; it's that great. The water lilies, bridges and streams, and the dreamlike way that the plants and natural geography come together are simply breathtaking. The "museum house" should definitely be visited as well, but is only open during the warmer months.

You can get there by all the usual methods of course and can certainly go there on your own but we do not encourage it. This is because a group tour offers one price and tons of convenience not to mention all of the fellow travelers you'll meet during the excursion. The folks at *Viator* not only make sure you have a comfortable journey, they also provide an art historian guide, give priority access to the house museum, and bypass many other expenses and annoyances compared with going there on your own. *Très belle!*

viator.com
(Main site page) Search: *Skip the line Giverny*

Their *skip-the-line* tour leaves from 2 Rue des Pyramides
(near the Louvre)
In the 1st arrondissement, Paris

(continued)

Daily departures are by luxury coach at 8:30am and 1:30pm
(April through October only)

Telephone contact will be given at time of confirmation
Email contact available directly through their website

A 24 hour cancellation refund is offered

Part 2

Connect with Nature
❖ Outdoor activities in and around Paris ❖

Some people are at their happiest when they're doing something outside. You know who you are. Here you'll find our top recommendations of outdoor activities in Paris. Not great at riding a bicycle? Try an electric scooter instead. Find something on our list that sounds like fun to you and then go for it.

Let "Horse in the City" arrange a ride you'll never forget

Go Horseback Riding
in the Bois de Boulogne

The Bois de Boulogne, a forest park and former hunting ground of kings located in a western section of Paris is the perfect place for a few hours on horseback. Now you can go for a lesson (even learning to ride side saddle) or just enjoy time with friends or family in a private horse ride with an experienced guide. The equestrian experts at "Horse in the City" will arrange everything, including instruction, snacks, or even a full picnic to compliment your experience. Contact them by phone or email in advance and they will take care of the rest. Incredible!

horseinthecity.fr

The meet-up location will be arranged when you book

Intl. calling: (011) 33 6 84 33 05 58
Local calling: 06 84 33 05 58

Email: infos@horseinthecity.fr

Private horse-riding tours can be arranged year 'round, weather permitting

Jog along an Abandoned
Elevated Railway Line

Moments spent in the out of doors, even a solitary moment, can be something special. If a morning jog or an urban hike is the way you like to start your day, we have just the spot. In the 19th century, an elevated train used to circle around Paris but was decommissioned long ago. The track remains however, along with some overgrown shrubbery, and gives runners a peaceful area in which to take their exercise. The part of the circular track that is still accessible lies north of the city center, through a gate at the location indicated below. The *Petite Ceinture,* as it is called, is one of Paris's truly wild spaces. It's a corridor for graffiti artists too and has an almost mythical reputation.

No official website

Entrance located at 101 Rue Olivier de Serres
You can access the old railway line here. Look for the green sign that says: *The Petite Ceinture of the 15th* (as in 15th arrondissement) posted on a silver gate. There's a glass elevator which you are welcome to use as well as a winding stairway to get to the deserted tracks.

Public space / Open daily

Try a Full Day Bike
Tour of Versailles

There's nothing to stop you from biking on your own all the way from Paris to Versailles and back again; it only takes about ninety minutes each way. But it's much more fun to join the English-speaking, small group tours from "Bike About" because they've thought of *everything*.

Join other fun-seekers at a café in the city center and then ride the train altogether to Versailles. From there you'll get on your bikes and see the village and palace in a way that most visitors never do. Not only will you explore the fabulous open market and quaint streets of the town, you'll be treated to a picnic feast right on the grounds of the royal châteaux. Next you'll explore Marie Antoinette's peasant village and be given time to see the palace. Go ahead; make the French countryside yours.

bikeabouttours.com

The meeting place is located at:
Le Peloton Café,
17 Rue du Point Louis Philippe
In the 4th arrondissement, Paris

Intl. calling: (011) 33 6 18 80 84 92
Local calling: 06 18 80 84 92

Email contact available directly through their website

Open daily during spring & summer
This experience lasts from 8:30am to 6pm

A 72 hour cancellation refund is offered

Tour the Monuments
on an Electric Scooter

Enjoy a day of fine weather by zipping through the streets of Paris on a seated or standing electric scooter (and we don't mean the Moped type.) You'll see more of the city's beautiful spaces and monuments this way than you ever could on foot. We rent ours from Rent&Go because they keep everything simple. If you've never tried an electric scooter then you don't know what you're missing. It's a blast!

rentngo.fr

Shops located at:
101 Avenue de la Bourdonnais
In the 7th arrondissement, Paris
or
19 Quai des Grands Augustins
In the 6th arrondissement, Paris

Intl. calling: (011) 33 6 32 97 33 11
Local calling: 06 32 97 33 11

Email contact available directly through their website

Open daily from 10:30am to 8pm
Closed on some major holidays

For a seamless rental, reserve your scooters ahead online

Have a Picnic in the City's Loveliest Green Space

Is there any better way to commune with nature than to picnic in a park? The word *pique-nique* is from the 1600's and is French in origin which shows you how long the Parisians have been doing it. Of course, Paris can be bitterly cold during the winter months so let's just say this one of our more seasonal suggestions.

Between the fabulous cheese shops, bakeries, and various *épicerie*, it's easy to put together a finger-food feast here. You could even just grab some fresh baguette sandwiches and something to drink and keep it simple.

Our favorite picnic spot is the gorgeous *Square du Vert-Galant*. This little park in the middle of the Seine enjoys sweeping views of both the Right and Left Banks. You'll find it at the western tippy-tip of Île de la Cité which means it's at the opposite end from Notre Dame Cathedral. Access this adorable green space from the Pont Neuf bridge and then go down the stairs near the back of the equestrian statue. (This all makes sense when you're there.)

If you're coming from the Right Bank, stop for picnic goodies at *Fromagerie Danard* at 5 Rue du Colonel Driant. If you're coming from the Left Bank, just grab some baguette sandwiches at *Paul Boulangerie* at 21 Rue de Buci. And since public consumption of alcohol is legal up until 9pm, don't forget to bring some wine and plastic cups to toast your beautiful day.

No website

Square du Vert-Galant, on Île de la Cité
In the 1st arrondissement, Paris

Public space/ always open

Splash in a Floating
Swimming Pool on the Seine

In 1785, a Monsieur Turquin opened the first swimming school at a pool that was installed on a floating barge docked in the Seine River. Soon after, there were many of them but today there's only one, the *Piscine Josephine Baker*. This large swimming pool east of the city center is open to the public and is quite popular. In addition to the four lane pool, there's a special one for babies, a solarium for sunbathing, Jacuzzi, saunas, aqua bikes, and a body building gym. Note that the Jacuzzi, saunas, and gym are not open at all times so check ahead.

Swimming caps are mandatory for both men and women and may be purchased there. Men and boys need to bring their Lycra swimwear because surf-short swimwear is prohibited. Bring your own bottled water in case you get thirsty. There's a small entrance fee, good for two hours at a time, and be sure to note that American Express is not one of the accepted credit cards. The pool is closed during certain local holidays so call ahead or check their website for the seasonally changing hours of operation. In summer it is open as late as 11pm.

piscine-baker.fr

Located at Quai François Mauriac
In the 13th arrondissement, Paris

Intl. calling: (011) 33 1 56 61 96 50
Local calling: 01 56 61 96 50

Email: contact@piscine-baker.fr

Changing seasonal hours so check their website for details

Rent a City Bike
during Sunset

Paris has some twenty-thousand Velib' bicycles ready to be rented on the cheap. You'll see them everywhere and you don't need a reservation. They can be rented for a day or a week during which they can be picked-up and dropped-off (or switched out) at different locations as many times as you want. This makes the entire system more convenient than renting from a shop.

The Velib' app makes the whole thing even easier so download it prior to renting your bike. Wait for sunset and then ride along the very bank of the Seine. Safety helmets are not mandatory in Paris so be sure to take care.

When you're done, return the bike to a docking station and be sure to take the printed receipt so you have proof that it made it back. Many of the Velib' bikes (both regular and electric) have a basket attached –just the thing for carrying delicious picnic items to your favorite park.

velib-metropole.fr/en

Online map of the docking locations:
velib-metropole.fr/en/map#

Intl. calling: (011) 33 1 76 49 12 34
Local calling: 01 76 49 12 34 (customer service)

Available 24/7
The electric bikes will have blue accents; the mechanical bikes will have green accents

(continued)

21

Complete your entire rental on the Velib' app, or in person using these instructions:

- At every docking station, there's a control podium. Using its simple instructions, (in English or French) sign-up for either a 24-hour pass (*V-Découverte*) or week-long pass (*V-Séjour.*) You will register your credit card and choose a pin number, after which a ticket will be printed with your personal subscription number. Keep this ticket.

- Every time you want to take a bike, simply go to the podium at the docking station and punch in your subscription number as well as your unique PIN number. Look over the bikes carefully and then enter the number of the one you want.

- Avoid bikes which are displaying a backwards seat as it has become a common courtesy to turn the seat around if there's anything wrong with it.

- Return your bike whenever you're finished; just insert it into any dock.

Visit the Eco-Friendly
Village Nature de Paris

Book a special stay for a couple of nights at *Village Nature de Paris*, a bit of heaven-on-Earth located just thirty minutes east of Paris, and just five minutes from the Paris Disneyland. Whether you want to include a visit to the famous theme park is a personal choice; there's plenty to see and do right in the *Village Nature*. Visitors can even purchase a day pass but it's much more fun to stay overnight.

This innovative resort uses only local and sustainable materials, foods, and water… literally a natural habitat for humans. You and your loved ones will reconnect in harmony with nature at this beautiful place.

Each of its five immersive worlds will provide a unique experience. These include the AquaLagoon, the Belle Vie Farm, the Extraordinary Gardens, the Forest of Legend & Secrets, and the Lakeside Promenade. There's even a beach, bicycling, bowling, ponies, zip-lines, cooking classes, bakeries, restaurants, and a luxury spa. You may never want to leave.

Reservations required

disneylandparis.com
(Main site page) click on: Places to Stay

Villages Nature Paris:
Located at Route de Villeneuve
In Bailly-Romainvilliers, France

Intl. calling: (011) 33 1 61 10 77 77
Local calling: 01 61 10 77 77
Email contact available directly through their website

Open year round
The "beach" area of the resort is open during summer

Disney's *Village Nature de Paris*

Part 3

Learn Something New
❖ And gain knowledge of the culture ❖

When you want to get a better understanding of the local culture here, don't take a class about Parisians...take a class *with* Parisians! From making your own croissants to learning about wine tasting or how to do make a hat from scratch, give one of these educational experiences a try. You will probably make a new Parisian friend in the process.

Learning about wine is fun because you get to drink it

Indulge in a
Wine Tasting Workshop

If you like French wine and feel you're ready to learn more about it, join this fun and informative wine tasting workshop held conveniently near the Louvre Museum. An English-speaking wine Sommelier will teach you how to identify and taste wine and introduce you to samples from the different regions of France. You will discover how to read a wine label and also learn the difference between the production of Champagne, Bordeaux, Sancerre, and Rhône wines. This French wine tasting "Tour de France" includes one Champagne, six French wines (from different regions,) a basket of bread, the Sommelier's presentation, Riedel glassware, a wine list, and a cheat sheet. *Santé!*

getyourguide.com
(Main site page) Search: *Paris*

Located at 68 Rue Jean-Jacques Rousseau
In the 1st arrondissement, Paris

Calling from the US or Canada: (1) 844-326-5840
Calling from Paris: 01 75 85 97 22 (customer service)

Email contact available directly through their website

Offered daily but must be booked online
Check availability on the calendar posted on the website above

A 24 hour cancellation refund is offered

Try a Lesson in French
Croissant-Making

Perhaps you've never considered baking your own French croissants, those flaky, buttery pastries that everyone loves. Our friends at *Le Foodist* cooking school will set you up right and show you just how to do it. Even if you never make croissants again, it's an eye-opening experience that will give you a new appreciation of them. Book ahead because these classes are popular, perhaps because they are taught in English.

lefoodist.com

Located at 59 Rue du Cardinal Lemoine
In the 5th arrondissement, Paris

Intl. calling: (011) 33 6 71 70 95 22
Local calling: 06 71 70 95 22

Email: contact@lefoodist.com

Open daily
Class schedule varies by subject
Check availability on the calendar posted on the website above

Take a Special Night Tour
of Le Musée du Louvre

You can book a two and a half hour walking tour of the Louvre with a private guide. Skip the line and enter one of the world's most amazing museums at night when the crowds of other visitors are gone. Your guide will present invaluable insight about the masterpieces like the infamous *Mona Lisa*. You'll hear the incredible stories *behind* the art and learn about the artists and their work. Because this is a private tour for just you and your loved ones it can even be personalized to the acquisitions that you're most interested in. Offered on Wednesday and Friday evenings only.

withlocals.com
(Main site page) Search: *Paris*

Meeting point:
Louvre Pyramid, near the front of the museum
Just off Rue de Rivoli
In the 1st arrondissement, Paris

Calling from the US or Canada:
(011) 31 20 24 40 076 or
(011) 31 20 2613 477
Calling from within France: (00) 31 20 2613 477

Email: hello@withlocals.com
Check availability on the website calendar above

Note: The entry tickets for the museum are not included but your guide will buy them for you in advance so you don't have to worry about it. This will save you time. (Just pay back your guide in cash at the beginning of the tour… around €17 per person.)

Free cancellation up to fourteen days before reserved date

Find Your Inner Julia
at Le Cordon Bleu

If you have a half-day free to do something truly amazing, try one of the many workshops offered at the world famous Le Cordon Bleu culinary school. The classes are taught by a real chef and include a demonstration, a tasting, and then execution with individual attention paid to all. When you're finished, you will feel confident to cook the dishes learned for your friends and family. You even get to take what you made with you so that you can start impressing someone right away. There's an English interpreter at every workshop just to make sure that nothing gets lost in translation. All levels of expertise are welcome, and that means you! C'mon, the bragging rights alone are off the chart. By the way, the menus created do change with what's in season at that time. Duh.

cordonbleu.edu/paris/home/en
(Main site page) Click on: *Culinary workshops*

Located at 13 Quai André Citroën
In the 15th arrondissement, Paris

Intl. calling: (011) 33 1 85 65 15 00
Local calling: 01 85 65 15 00
Email contact available directly through their website

Note: Workshops in categories ranging from "The Art of Cooking Like a Chef" to simply Macarons, Chocolate, Breadbaking, Sauces, and Pastries are ongoing and each have their own calendar (posted on the website.) The less expensive of the "Chef" workshops is a demonstration only, so if you want to do some cooking yourself as we describe above, be sure to choose the one that's around €195.00.

Their different class categories range from two to six hours long.

Create an Original Fragrance
at a French Perfumery

Is there anything as *très chic* as creating your own original fragrance with a French perfume expert? We think not. Spend ninety minutes exploring base oils as you learn what affects the top and bottom notes of the scent... you will leave with a bottle of your new *parfum* and will learn tons in the process. In addition, they will keep your exact formula on file so that you can reorder it online anytime. Why smell like everybody else? The lovely specialists at either *Le Studio des Parfum* or at *Atelier de Création de Parfum Candora* will make sure you leave their class contented. Both studios are conveniently located in the city center on the Right Bank.

Check availability on website calendars below

Le Studio des Parfums:

studiodesparfums-paris.fr
(Main site page) Click on: *Customized Fragrance Workshop*

Located at 23 Rue du Bourg Tibourg
In the 4th arrondissement, Paris

Intl. calling: (011) 33 1 40 29 90 84
Local calling: 01 40 29 90 84

Email: info@sdp-paris.com

Open Monday through Saturday from 11am to 7pm
Closed Sundays and major holidays

(continued)

Atelier de Création de Parfum Candora:

candora-fragrance.com
(Main site page) Click on: *Perfume Creation Workshops*

Located at 1 Rue du Pont Louis-Philippe
In the 4th arrondissement, Paris

Intl. calling: (011) 33 1 43 48 76 05
Local calling: 01 43 48 76 05

Email: contact@candora.fr

Open Monday through Saturday from 2pm to 7pm
Closed Sundays and major holidays

Learn to Make
Classic French Desserts

Think you could never bake desserts as beautiful as the ones in the best restaurants? Think again. The English-speaking professionals at *Le Foodist* cooking school will take you through the process and let you taste their exceptional creations. Chocolate soufflé, Crêpes Suzette, Crème Brûlée, and Madeleines are all included in their class titled *Classical French Desserts*. It might just make you a star in your own kitchen. Book ahead because the classes are not large and fill up quickly.

lefoodist.com
(Main site page) Click on: *Classic French Desserts*

Located at 59 Rue du Cardinal Lemoine
In the 5th arrondissement, Paris

Intl. calling: (011) 33 6 71 70 95 22
Local calling: 06 71 70 95 22

Email: contact@lefoodist.com / lefoodist@hotmail.com

Open daily
Class schedule varies by subject

Check availability on the calendar posted on the website above

Take a Workshop
of Parisian Hat-Making

Sometimes you see a hat you really like but it doesn't fit your head. Instead of running all over Paris trying on hats, join this fun workshop where you will create (with an expert hat-maker) your own hat from scratch that will fit perfectly. In an atelier on the Right Bank, you'll choose all the elements of your hat including the material, shape, color, and embellishment. Ribbons, scarves, buttons, embroideries, and feathers are all provided to help inspire your creativity. The experience takes three hours, includes beverages, and is offered for men, women, and teens!

minime-paris.com/chapellerie

"Chapellerie/Patisserie MiniMe"
Located at 75 Boulevard e Sébastopol (2nd floor)
In the 2nd arrondissement, Paris

Intl. calling: (011) 33 1 40 15 96 84
Local calling: 01 40 15 96 84

Email contact available directly through their website

Classes are held daily
Closed on major holidays

Check availability on their website calendar

A 24 hour cancellation refund is offered

Enjoy Cheese & Wine Pairings
in a 17th Century Cellar

Are you curious about French wines and cheeses and the connection they share with each other? Learn everything you need to know at a "wine and cheese pairings" workshop at Paroles des Fromagers. You will learn how to choose the cheeses and which goes with what and why. An English-speaking, expert cheesemonger will introduce you to the science of tasting and pairing. There are different workshops to choose from but we like the one where they include nine aged cheeses and four French wines inside an actual 17th century tasting cellar. They call it a science, we call it an art.

parolesdefromagers.com/en
(Main site page)

Located at 41 Rue du Faubourg du Temple
In the 10th arrondissement, Paris

Intl. calling: (011) 33 6 85 57 76 52
Local calling: 06 85 57 76 52

Open Mondays from 4pm to 8:30pm
Open Tuesday through Friday from 10am to 1pm,
   and 4pm to 8:30pm
Open Saturdays from 10am to 8:30pm
Closed Sundays and major holidays

Check availability on their website calendar

Part 4

Search for Something
❖ Hunting for Parisian goodies is fun ❖

Folks born with the *collector's gene* know precisely what we're suggesting here, but probing through an ancient city for that special something can be a fascinating experience for anyone. From antiquing to couture, and craft shops to flea markets, we've got you covered. If your special skill happens to be shopping, this is your chapter.

Treasure hunting in Paris can be an unending preoccupation

Shop the Paris Flea Market with a Connoisseur

Have you previously dipped a toe into the city's famous flea market and found you didn't much like it? That's because you didn't know precisely where to find what you were looking for. If you're like other visitors to Paris, you probably only saw a tiny fraction of the sprawling area anyway. Do yourself a favor and go shopping there *again*, but this time with a connoisseur of vintage and antique items who really knows the layout of the place. This wonderful, guided shopping experience lasts two hours.

pariscityvision.com/en/flea-market-tour

Meeting place is at the Église Notre-Dame du Rosaire church,
65 Avenue Gabriel Péri
Saint-Ouen, France (just outside of the Paris boundary)

Email contact available directly through their website

This experience is offered on Saturdays and Sundays because that's when Paris' most famous flea market is open. Note that it is always closed during the month of August

Check availability on the calendar posted on the website above
A 48 hour cancellation refund is offered

Métro Line 13 to the Garibaldi station

Take a Private Shopping Trip
with a Parisian Stylist

Discover the cutest shops and the latest trends with your very own Parisian stylist. A knowledgeable personal shopper will advise you as you browse through the quaint Marais neighborhood and beyond. This private, two hour experience will make you feel like a true fashion insider in the City of Lights. They will stick to *your* budget and even show you some really great affordable clothing. Because you are unique, everything will be customized around your preferred look.

viator.com
(Main site page) Search: *Paris Personal Shopper*

Meeting place located at Filles du Calvaire
In the 11th arrondissement, Paris

Calling from the US or Canada: (1) 855-818-6895
Calling from Paris: (001) 855-818-6895

Email contact available directly through their website

This experience is offered on most days
Reservation required/ meet times are flexible

Check availability on the calendar posted on the website above

No cancellation refund once it's booked.

Weigh in on Fashion
at the Kilo Shop

Do you just adore fashion treasure hunting? If so, head over to one of the city's Kilo Shops. These fun second-hand clothing boutiques are found in several neighborhoods but we like the one in Saint-Germain-des-Prés. Check those designer labels but don't look for any price tags…just grab whatever you want and then take it to be weighed. At the Kilo store, you pay by weight! You might not find anything vintage on the day you visit but you never know. That perfect Givenchy trouser just might be waiting for you.

kilo-shop.com/en
(Main site page)

Located at 125 Boulevard Saint-Germain
In the 6th arrondissement, Paris

Intl. calling: (011) 33 1 43 26 00 36
Local calling: 01 43 26 00 36

Email contact available directly through their website

Open Monday through Saturday from 11am to 7:30pm
Closed Sundays and major holidays

Visit a Shop that's Bursting
with Upcycled Goods

You've heard of recycling, but what about upcycling? This is the art of taking unwanted or unneeded items and making them into something completely new instead of simply discarding them. Only in Paris will you find *LaBeL RéCuP'* –a somewhat hidden boutique stuffed with an eclectic collection of upcycled items for the home or the bohemian wardrobe. We say it's the wave of the future; you'll just say wow!

No official website

Located at 27 Rue de la Folie Méricourt
In the 1st arrondissement Paris

Intl. calling: (011) 33 9 53 96 41 46
Local calling: 09 53 96 41 46

Email contact available directly through their website

Open Tuesday through Sunday from 11am to 8pm
Open Sundays from 3pm to 6pm only
Closed Mondays and some major holidays

See the Top Fashion Boutiques
of the Golden Triangle

When nothing but the best will do, go for a little shopping spree or browse-fest in the haute couture neighborhood west of the Louvre. There you'll be seduced by Europe's top designers which are all to be found in the so-called *Triangle d'Or*. World famous shops are scattered throughout this area on the Right Bank just north of the Jardin des Tuileries.

The Avenue Montaigne, Avenue Georges V, Rue St Honoré, Rue du Faubourg Saint-Honoré, Avenue des Champs-Élysées, Rue de Rivoli, and Place Vendôme all play home to flagship stores. You'll see boutiques like Dior, Chloé, Celine, Prada, Ferragamo, Valentino, Jean-Paul Gaultier, Givenchy, Saint Laurent, Versace, Louis Vuitton, Goyard, Chanel, and Hermès. Don't be afraid, you don't *have* to buy anything... but it's more fun if you do.

Most of the boutiques are open Monday through Saturday
from 11am to 7pm

Check with specific boutiques for their special opening hours
All are closed on major holidays

Peruse through France's
Oldest Flea Market

If you're the independent type that appreciates a unique find and likes to discover it without any help from others, then head over to the area's oldest flea market. The *Saint-Ouen* flea market, known simply as *Clignancourt* or *Les Puces*, is actually twelve flea markets in one area. It began in 1870 and is both indoor and outdoor, with several thousand stalls in all, making it the largest vintage and antique market in the world. That makes it "goodies central."

Nowadays it also offers items that are more touristy than vintage, including tee shirts, and trinkets for visitors from abroad. But if you can find the original section, the winding alleyways of the *Marchés Vernsaison,* then you just might find that crazy, historic item you've been dreaming of. Going there in the morning is best for this kind of treasure hunting because the best things will not yet be taken, and the hoards of shoppers it attracts will still be at breakfast. Don't be afraid to negotiate the price of something; pretend to walk away like you're not going to buy it and see what happens.

Finally, be safe, and keep your valuables secured. Don't bring your passport, and be aware of your surroundings. The area of the flea market is perfectly safe but there can be pickpockets. Use the map on your smart phone to find Rue des Rosiers; it will save you from just wandering around when you could be seeing the better stuff.

marcheauxpuces-saintouen.com

(continued)

44

Located along Rue des Rosiers
Just outside Paris' 18th arrondissement,
in Saint-Ouen, France

Open Saturdays from 9am to 6pm
Open Sundays from 10am to 6pm
Open seasonally on Mondays from 11am to 5pm
(Note: Many stalls close for a bit during lunch time)

Closed during the month of August

Go Antiquing
on the Left Bank

If you think flea markets are nasty and prefer to browse in proper antique stores, then head for the *Village Suisse*. This pedestrian-only shopping configuration is actually a cluster of stores that take up an entire block. Close to the Eiffel Tower, it boasts a hundred antique stores as well as art galleries and modern home décor shops. If you're a collector of beautiful things, this is your place.

Bring along your passport in case you buy something pricy so that you can register for the visitors' VAT tax refund. (Note that some antique items do not qualify for this.) From chandeliers to carousel horses, these shops are definitely worth your time…whether you're there to buy something or not. Small gardens and patios are sprinkled throughout to give shoppers a place for a much-needed break.

villagesuisse.com

Entrances on both Avenue de Suffren and on Avenue de la Motte-Picquet
In the 15th arrondissement, Paris

Email contact available directly through their website

Open Thursday through Monday from 10:30am to 7pm
Open on Public Holidays
Closed on Tuesdays and Wednesdays

Visit the Most Beautiful
Wine Store in Paris

Tucked inside the magnificent arcade of *Galerie Vivienne*, the wine store called "Legrand Filles et Fils" is no joke. It takes up both sides of a gorgeous mosaic courtyard and offers one of the city's best selections of French wines from Burgundy and the Loire Valley, including the infamous *Beaujolais*. They also have a restaurant, wine-tasting, a charcuterie counter, and other treats to purchase. You can grab a great deal here but remember that you could be taxed a couple of bucks on each liter bottle (after the one that's allowed without taxation) by US customs. Of course, no one is stopping you from enjoying a bottle or two before you leave Europe.

caves-legrand.com

Located at 1 Rue de la Banque
In the 2nd arrondissement, Paris
– inside the *Galerie Vivienne*

Intl. calling: (011) 33 1 42 60 07 12
Local calling: 01 42 60 07 12

Email: info@caves-legrand.com

Open Mondays from 11am to 7pm
Open Tuesday through Saturday from 10am to 7:30pm
Closed Sundays and major holidays

Part 5

Have an Engrossing Individual Experience
❖ Make it all about you ❖

When you're in need some real *me time*, one of the amazing suggestions below should fit the bill. Whether you crave total relaxation or are willing to make some risky decisions, you'll definitely enjoy at least one of the experiences in this chapter. Go to Paris and return home a different person.

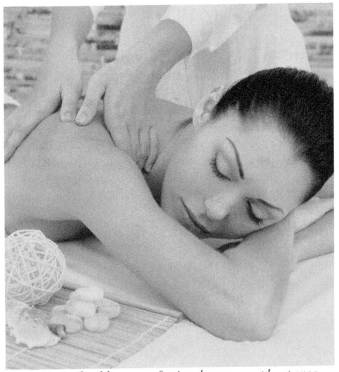

Everyone should try a professional massage at least once

Surrender to a Half-Day French Spa Experience

Fashion designer and icon Christian Dior believed that happiness could come from beauty. Here at the *Dior Institut* spa, beauty is what they do. Both women and men are welcome here, and pampered beyond imagination through a series of dedicated treatments. Their offerings are top notch to be sure, and there's an extensive list to choose from. You can simply select the type of treatment or massage you're most interested in, or you can speak to one of the Dior specialists to help you decide. The *Dior Institut* is housed inside the Plaza Athénée Paris but you don't have to be a guest at the hotel to book a spa appointment.

dorchestercollection.com/en
(Main site page) Search: *Paris*

Located at 25 Avenue Montaigne
In the 8th arrondissement, Paris

Intl. calling: (011) 33 1 53 67 65 35
Local calling: 01 53 67 65 35

Email: info.HPA@dorchestercollection.com

April through October:
Open daily from 9:30am to 9pm
Closed on major holidays

November through March
Open daily from 10:30am to 8pm
Closed on major holidays

Check availability on the calendar posted on the website above

Learn Salsa Dancing
the French Way

Sometimes you just need to take a Salsa class, right? When your body feels the need to make some moves but yoga seems a bit sedate, take a class with the friendly dance instructors at Salsabor Paris. Not only will you have a great time, you'll work off some of those croissants you ate. By the way, if the Salsa is not really your fave, choose a class from the many other dance disciplines offered at this wonderful school in the city center. Everyone is welcome!

salsabor.fr/nos-cours

Located at 31 Rue Chapon
In the 3rd arrondissement, Paris

Intl. calling: (011) 33 1 42 71 61 61
Local calling: 01 42 71 61 61

Email: contact@salsabor.fr

Open Monday through Saturday from 1pm to 10pm
Closed Sundays and major holidays

Experience the "Pure Chocolate" Walking Tour

Does your heart flutter wildly at the very thought of chocolate? If so, we have the walking tour for you. Stroll the Right Bank with an expert guide as you savor and sample artisan treats from five of Paris' master chocolatiers. During the two hour experience you'll also learn about the ubiquitous cocoa bean, which makes this experience educational as well. (We put that there in case one of your loved ones gives you a hard time for choosing a chocolate tour.)

getyourguide.com/paris-l16/pure-chocolate-walking-tour-t4599

Meeting place located at 3 Place de la Madeleine
In the 8th arrondissement, Paris

"GetYourGuide" tour company
Calling from the US or Canada: (1) 844-326-5840
Calling from the UK: 44 (0) 20 3962 0237
Local calling from within Paris: 01 75 85 97 22

Email contact available directly through their website

Tours offered Monday through Saturday
Reservation required
Closed Sundays and major holidays

Available to everyone age six and older
Check availability on their website calendar

A 48 hour cancellation refund is offered

Admire Art in a Preserved
19th Century Mansion

In the northwest section of Paris there is a magnificent townhouse that is perfectly preserved and *not* full of tourists. The living museum called *Musée Jacquemart-André* is right on the famous Boulevard Haussmann and is definitely worth your time. It will leave you in awe, especially if you appreciate artwork and all the finer things in life.

Built in 1860, this exquisite home showcases art from as early as the 15th century in rooms that are gloriously decorated. There's even a garden and a beautiful café where you can have lunch. We think it's perfect.

musee-jacquemart-andre.com

Located at 158 Boulevard Haussmann
In the 8th arrondissement, Paris

Intl. calling: (011) 33 1 45 62 11 59
Local calling: 01 45 62 11 59

Email contact available directly through their website

Open daily from 10am to 5:30pm (entry time)
May close on major holidays so call ahead

Critique Avant-Garde Photography
at the Jeu de Paume

Do you have an interest (and perhaps some real talent) in recognizing great photography? Are you fascinated by modern art but have loved ones who could care less about it? If you're one of those special people with a discerning eye, then treat yourself to an hour or two at the *Galerie Nationale du Jeu de Paume*. This neo-classical building at the corner of the Tuileries garden used to house the royal tennis courts back in the day. Now it's the center of modern and post-modern photography in Paris.

Don't take anyone with you; they might spoil it. Just go by yourself and have what could very well be a transporting personal experience. Some things have no language barrier.

jeudepaume.org

Located at 1 Place de la Concorde
In the 1st arrondissement, Paris

Intl. calling: (011) 33 1 47 03 12 50
Local calling: 01 47 03 12 50

Email: accueil@jeudepaume.org

Open Tuesday through Friday from noon to 8pm
Open Saturdays & Sundays from 11am to 8pm
Closed on Mondays and some major holidays

Benefit from a One-on-One Styling Experience

Get styled in Paris! Book a three hour shopping experience with an English-speaking fashion expert who will take you on a private, personal shopping adventure in the Marais, Montmartre, Saint-Germain-des-Prés, or even the Golden Triangle of top designer boutiques. It's your choice. It includes a complimentary beverage break so you can catch your second wind. Not only will you end up with some amazing finds, you will discover shops and streets you didn't know you loved so much. Bring some friends along if you want because it can accommodate up to seven people.

localers.com/our-tours-in-Paris
(Main site page) Enter your dates for more info

Meeting place located outside the Saint-Paul Métro Station
In the 4th arrondissement, Paris

Calling from the US or Canada: (1) 888-460-3512
Local calling from within Paris: 01 83 64 92 01

Email: booking@localers.com

This experience is offered Tuesday through Saturday
Reservation required, meet times are flexible

Check availability on their website calendar

A 48 hour cancellation refund is offered

Find Your New Haircut
in a Paris Salon

A fantastic haircut can be a transforming thing for both men and women. Get a completely new look at Sequence Paris, a respected (but not snooty) hair salon located in a narrow street on the Left Bank. Their prices are very fair and they speak perfect English, an important consideration when you want your new look to be how you imagined it. There are many hair salons in Paris but this is the one to trust. They specialize in color too and can even pull off a great *ombre*. Children are welcome as well.

Appointments can be made right on their website

sequenceparis.com

Located at 13 Rue des Lyonnais
In the 5th arrondissement

Intl. calling: (011) 33 6 62 84 47 72
Local calling: 06 62 84 47 72

Email: contact@sequenceparis.com

Opens Tuesday through Saturday at 10am
Late hours offered on Thursday & Friday
Closed on Sundays & Mondays and major holidays

Métro Line 7 to the Censier-Daubenton station

Challenge Yourself in a
Paris Running Event

Parisians love to run and their city has so many organized running events that there's now a year round calendar to explore (at the website listed below.) Pick one that catches your fancy, or that matches up with the dates of your visit. Then just register and join the fun.

If you prefer to run in a smaller group, try one of the private or semi-private events offered up by Paris Running Tours. Either way, treat yourself to an éclair *and* a cream puff afterwards.

parisrunningtour.com/races

Running tours and running events, located in the city center
Paris

Intl. calling: (011) 33 6 02 11 52 10
Local calling: 06 02 11 52 10

Email contact available directly through their website

Dates and times vary
Check details on the calendar posted on the website above

Become the Art with a
Permanent Souvenir

Grab some ink and return home with a souvenir from the Body Staff Tattoo Shop. This highly respected and creative shop near the Bois de Vincennes is where locals get their ink on. Because of its location in Vincennes they can offer clients a better price, and appointment times that you don't have to wait weeks for (like those tattoo shops in the city center.) Body Staff enjoys a spectacular reputation and, along with its regular staff, brings in artists from around the world to guest there for weeks at a time. Our advice? Choose a design that you really love and can live with.

Afterwards, take a peek at the nearby 14th century castle and tower called the Château de Vincennes It lies just south of the Métro station there.

body-staff.com

**Located at 45 Rue Robert Giraudineau
In Vincennes, France**

Intl calling: (011) 33 1 41 93 14 13
Local calling: 01 41 93 14 13

Email: latikbou@body-staff.com

Open Monday through Saturday from 10am-7pm
Call ahead to reserve a time

Métro Line 1 to the Château de Vincennes station

Part 6

Make Memories
❖ **Share delightful moments with loved ones** ❖

Some things in Paris are best when shared. Whether you want to plan a special celebration or unique experience for yourself and a loved one, or for *everyone* in your party, we've got you covered. The places on this list will make all of them forget about their smart phones and give everyone something to really talk about. This is also where you'll find our curated recommendations for Paris' most unusual dining spots.

There are many types of wine and cheese experiences in Paris

Taste Wines
with an Expert

Okay, so you know about wine and want to further your knowledge with a tasting in Paris. The problem is that you want to bring your loved one along and spend more time enjoying the wine rather than hearing a lecture. Wine expert Michel will meet you and your party for a custom wine tasting and pairing experience inside a typical Parisian wine bar that just happens to feature natural, organic artisan wines. After three hours of gourmet nibbles, cheese, and at least six different wines, you'll definitely know what's what.

withlocals.com/experience/d9803675

Meeting place is near Saint-Paul du Marais
In the 4th arrondissement, Paris

This completely customizable, private experience is offered on most days, and the meet times are flexible.

Check availability by contacting Michel, the host, through the WithLocals website above

Be Spellbound by
Immersive Digital Art

We're just going to say it: don't miss the new *L'Atelieres des Lumières,* the first digital arts center in Paris. This unique museum offers an immersive experience that lets you enjoy famous works of art through projections and sound. Translated as "Workshops of Light," we think it is actually much, much more than that. Stand in awe as a giant, digitized van Gogh sweeps over your body. Hold your breath as a famous painting fills the entire room and moves about in a 3D formation! Their creative team has invented something really new and you deserve to experience it. Book your ticket ahead because it frequently sells out, and with good reason.

atelier-lumieres.com/en

Located at 38 Rue Saint-Maur
In the 11th arrondissement, Paris

Intl. calling: (011) 33 1 80 98 46 00
Local calling: 01 80 98 46 00

Email contact available directly through their website

**Open Monday through Thursday from 10am to 5:15pm
(entry times)**
**Open Fridays & Saturdays from 10am to 9:15pm
(entry times)**
Open Sundays from 10am to 6:15pm (entry times)
Closed on some major holidays so call ahead

Indulge at a
Parisian Jazz Club

Since Paris is the birthplace of jazz it seems only right to send you over to our favorite jazz club, Duc des Lombards. One of *many* jazz joints in town, Duc's is as real as it gets and has less of the glitz and frou-frou that the fancier ones flaunt. Its acoustics are top notch, allowing guests to really feel the music. Piano and saxophone rule here so go kick up your heels. Conveniently located in the center of town, you'll find your way home just fine even if you overindulge. This prestigious club has been swinging since 1984.

ducdeslombards.com

Located at 42 Rue des Lombard
In the 1st arrondissement, Paris

Intl. calling: (011) 33 1 42 33 22 88
Local calling: 01 42 33 22 88

Email: contact@ducdeslombards.com

Open Monday through Thursday from 7pm to 11:30pm
Open Fridays & Saturdays from 7pm to 3:30am
Closed Sundays and major holidays

Dine in Absolute Darkness
at Restaurant "Dans le Noir"

A sensual foodie experience can be had at a small restaurant over by the Pompidou Centre of Modern Art. People say that when your sight is completely inhibited, the food you are eating takes on a more intense flavor and appreciation. At *L'espace Sensoriel- Dans le Noir*, guests are guided to their tables by members of the blind staff and served an exquisite meal in a room that is pitch dark. You'll have to guess what you're eating, which is part of the fun. Now a worldwide phenomenon, this location in Paris was the very first in *blind dining*.

When you make the requisite reservation, mention any food sensitivities of the people in your party so that the chef can accommodate it. This is definitely a dining experience you will never forget.

Reservations necessary

sens.danslenoir.com

Located at 40 Rue Quincampoix
In the 4th arrondissement, Paris

Intl. calling: (011) 33 9 83 49 87 97
Local calling: 09 83 49 87 97

Email contact available directly through their website

Open Tuesday through Saturday from 11am to 8pm
Closed Sundays and Mondays, and some major holidays
Hours may vary in the off-season

Order up a Romantic, Professionally-Catered Picnic

Do you love a picnic but don't like having to put one together? Perhaps you want to plan a surprise. No problem. Picnicking is considered an art form in this city and for the best one of your life, all you have to do is go online and click. A gorgeous spread of goodies will arrive in the park or setting of your choice. We think their name says it all. At "Love Picnics," absolutely everything is done for you and all *you* have to do is relax, eat, drink, and enjoy.

lovepicnicparis.com

Located at 55 rue Réaumur
In the 2nd arrondissement, Paris

Intl. calling: (011) 33 6 24 96 71 57
Local calling: 06 24 96 71 57

Email: info@lovepicnicparis.com

Lunchtime delivery available between 12:30pm and 1pm
Evening delivery available between 6pm and 7pm
Surprise deliveries are available!

Be Tempted by the Ubiquitous Apple at Restaurant Pomze

Adam and Eve never had it so good. Guests at Restaurant Pomze are served apple at every course, even in the desserts and cocktails, and it's sublime. You'll find it one level above the street inside a gorgeous Haussmann apartment building not far from the *Gare Saint-Lazare* train terminal. Throughout the year, over a hundred varieties of apples are used in their dishes. The menu changes about ten times a year, based on which style of apple is available rather than on the four seasons. Everything is there is made from the best products and produce available, even their lovely ciders. Both a la carte and prix fix menus are available for lunch and dinner. Be tempted!

Here is an excerpt from a recent seasonal menu:
Salad of grilled apricots, apples, crispy halloumi and parma ham
Fried green apples with freekeh salad and shrimp remoulade
Grilled bass with vegetables, tomato confit and apple cider butter
Beef tenderloin with radish chimichurri, green apples, and potatoes

pomze.com (Reservations recommended)

Located at 109 Boulevard Haussmann
In the 8th arrondissement, Paris

Intl calling: (011) 33 1 42 65 65 83
Local calling: 01 42 65 65 83
Email: contact@pomze.com

Serving Monday through Friday from noon to 2pm & 7pm to 9:30pm
Serving on Saturdays from 7pm to 9:30pm

Closed Sundays
Closed annually from December 22nd through January 2nd

Have a Professional
Photo Shoot around Town

Talk about making memories! Nothing can do it better than having professional photos of you and your loved ones that you'll cherish for *the rest of your life*. Understand this: these are nothing like selfies or casual group shots made with your smart phone. The resulting pictures from a photo shoot done by the professionals at "My Paris Photo" will look amazing and you will look amazing in them. Totally worth an hour or two of your time, and it's actually fun.

myparisphototour.com

Office located at 11 Bis Rue Sainte Anne
In the 1st arrondissement, Paris

Intl. calling: (011) 33 6 48 54 38 91
Local calling: 06 48 54 38 91

Email: info@myparisphototour.com

Photo shoots are available everyday depending on availability
Check open dates through the website above

Dine Inside the Oldest Building in Paris

Have you wondered which of the buildings on those Paris streets is the oldest? We know the answer. There's an old stone structure in the third arrondissement that dates back to 1407. It was built by the famous alchemist, Nicolas Flamel, and he and his wife resided there for some time, even after he turned lead into pure gold. That old book he found sure came in handy, teaching him how to create the Philosopher's Stone that made the miracle possible. (We can't make this stuff up.)

Throughout the centuries, the Flamel building almost always housed a tavern on its street level. Today it features a different kind of alchemy: the "cuisine du chef" of the restaurant *Auberge Nicolas Flamel.*

First you'll notice the strange façade, unchanged since the 15th century, carved over with markings and passages in Latin. The restaurant's interior does not have the same antique style but does serves incredible gastronomy, and gives you the bragging rights of having dined in such a place. Credit cards and gold coins accepted.

auberge-nicolas-flamel.fr *(Reservations recommended)*

Located at 51 Rue de Montmorency
In the 3rd arrondissement, Paris

Intl. calling: (011) 33 1 42 71 77 78
Local calling: 01 42 71 77 78
Email: auberge.flamel@yahoo.fr

Open daily from noon to 2:30pm, and from 7pm to 10:30pm
Closed on major holidays so call ahead

Chill Out at the Frozen "Ice Kube" Bar

Yes, there's an ice lounge in Paris and if you've never been to one then this is your chance. Like having cocktails inside a storage container in the tundra, this unique bar offers a very cold thirty minute experience that includes two drinks and a shot for a set price. Designed to be a frozen remnant of a post-apocalyptic world, thirty tons of ice was used to create the Ice Kube Bar. While not as large as ice bars in other cities, it's still worth the Uber trip to the 18th arrondissement. You must don jackets and gloves for the visit.

The bar itself is part of the city's Kube Hotel which also carries over on the post apocalypse theme. Head down the cobbled pathway off Rue Marx Dormoy and go through the unmarked grey entrance doors to find both the hotel and the bar.

kubehotel-paris.com *(Reservations recommended)*

Located at 5 Passage Ruelle
In the 18th arrondissement, Paris

Intl. calling: (011) 33 1 42 05 20 00
Local calling: 01 42 05 20 00

Email: kubeparis@machefert.com

Open nightly from 6:30pm to 1am
Closed during the month of August

Métro Line 2 to the San Chapelle station

Have Dinner on the
Eiffel Tower

What could be more Parisian than this? Whether you're looking for a special place to celebrate an occasion or want to have a meal that you'll never forget, book a table 400 feet above the Earth at *Le Jules Verne* for a five or six course tasting menu. This incredible restaurant located on the second level of the tower offers more than just great views. It is stunning in every way, and you'll be very happy that we sent you there. Note that it is often booked for weeks in advance so you need to plan ahead. (Once in a while you can snag a table that has canceled at the last minute…it never hurts to call and ask.)

Reservations necessary
Book through the calendar posted on the website below

The dress code is smart casual. No t-shirts, shorts, or trainers accepted.

restaurants-toureiffel.com
(Main site page) Click on Le Jules Verne

Located at the Eiffel Tower on **Avenue Gustave Eiffel**
In the 7th arrondissement, Paris

Intl. calling: (011) 33 1 45 55 61 44
Local calling: 01 45 55 61 44
Email contact available directly through their website

Open daily from noon to 1:30pm, and from 6pm to 9.30pm
Closed annually on July 14th for Bastille Day

To access this restaurant, take the private elevator located in the south pillar entrance of the Eiffel Tower. There is a private valet available for those with their own vehicle.

Métro Line 6 to the Bir-Hakeim-Grenelle station

Take a Champagne Cruise
on the River Seine

There's nothing like a night cruise on the Seine with Champagne to set you right again. Our friends at *Vedettes du Pont Neuf* offer just such a thing, complete with a full service bar and snacks. Their terraced boats are delightful and add to the romantic atmosphere. Marvel at the lights of Paris from quite a different perspective and wonder how anyone could ever be bored in such a city.

vedettesdupontneuf.com

Located at *Square du Vert Galant*
(On Île de la Cité at Pont Neuf)
In the 1st arrondissement, Paris

Intl. calling: (011) 33 1 46 33 98 38
Local calling: 01 46 33 98 38

Email: info@vedettesdupontneuf.com

Departures offered at 7pm or 9pm nightly

Check availability on the ir website calendar

Attend a Performance at the Magnificent Palais Garnier

There's only one *real* Paris Opera House and this is it. Its interiors are famous for a reason; they are the most opulent we've ever seen anywhere. The place even inspired the Phantom of the Opera… so while it's definitely worth a look by taking the self-tour with audio guide during the day, why not plan ahead and see like it should be seen: by attending a performance. Tickets for the opera, the ballet, or even various concerts are available year round through their website. While they often sell out, you can snag one if you do it far enough in advance of your dates. During intermission, be sure to visit its mind-blowing Grand Foyer. Superb!

operadeparis.fr/en

Located at Place de l'Opéra
In the 9th arrondissement, Paris

Intl. calling: (011) 33 1 71 25 24 23

Tickets can be booked directly through their website, or in person

Performance dates and times vary

Attempt to Find the
Entrance of a Speakeasy

Don't you just love finding a secret bar with a "hidden" entrance that's open late and serves good mixology? We do. And if you've never been to a speakeasy before, you should try it. In Paris that means an intimate bar lounge quietly hiding behind a working laundromat in the tenth arrondissement. Look for the "Lavomatic" at the address below and you're almost there. Now just find the way in…

It's not a large place and they don't take reservations so be prepared to wait on the weekends.

www.lavomatic.paris

Located at 30 rue René Boulanger
In the 10th arrondissement, Paris

No phone
This place is secret!

Open Tuesdays & Wednesdays from 6pm to 1am
Open Thursday through Saturday from 6pm to 2am
Closed Sundays & Mondays

Part 7

Local Thrills & Chills
❖ Some of Paris' more hair-raising sights ❖

We know that some people are just not happy unless they're doing something intense, spooky, or thrilling. If that describes you, then you're in luck. Activities in this chapter are definitely made to take your breath away and get your blood pumping, one way or another.

France is well known for its love of hot air balloons

Take a Spectacular Hot Air Balloon over Fontainebleau

If soaring silently over the Earth in a hot air balloon has ever been your dream, make it come true while you're in France. This sport is offered up by experts in many regions of the country but why not try it over a magnificent palace of kings? The Château de Fontainebleau boasts a surrounding countryside that's lush and green, and the area is easily reached by direct train from Paris' Gare de Lyon terminal. We think it's the ideal spot for an extraordinary ballooning experience. The skilled professionals at *France Montgolfières* will take good care of you and will even have you help with the before and after process of the ride. Afterwards, you and the pilot will toast to your flight with a glass of sparkling wine. C'mon, you know you want to do this!

france-balloons.com

Meeting place is at the Château de Fontainebleau
In Fontainebleau, France

To call from the US or Canada: 1-347-809-5371
To call from the U.K. +(44) 20 7097 5781
Local calling from within Paris: 03 80 97 38 61

Email contact available directly through their website

Flights are offered daily, April through October
Both daybreak and sunset flights are offered

Note: Open-date tickets can be purchased on their website. You can snag a last minute flight by calling a day or two before, especially on weekdays.

Ride on Creepy Carnival
Attractions from the 1800's

Inside a row of deserted wines cellars east of the city center lies a strange and wonderful museum unlike any other. The *Musée des Arts Forains* (Museum of Fairgrounds) boasts the antique collection of one man – and only houses part of it, at that. We like to think it's the best part. A guided tour of this mind-bending museum must be arranged by reservation only because it is completely interactive. Jean-Paul Favand is delighted to have you ride his rides and play the games which are all salvaged from old carnivals, circuses, and sideshows.

The dimly lit cellars reverberate with music from actual pipe organs as you make your way back in time. You'll see mechanical fortune tellers, ride a carousel from 1900, and experience a very rare self-pedaled bicycle ride just to name a few. This museum is beautiful yet creepy and is sure to raise the hairs on the back of your neck. Tickets must be purchased in advance coinciding with the various dates of the tours posted on their website. Even though this is not in our kids' section, children are welcome to join this unusual ninety-minute tour.

arts-forains.com

Located at 53 Avenue des Terroirs de France
In the 12th arrondissement, Paris
Housed inside the pointed-roofed buildings of *Les Pavillons de Bercy*

Intl. calling: (011) 33 1 43 40 16 22
Local calling: 01 43 40 16 22
Email: infos@pavillons-de-bercy.com

(continued)

By reservation only, at least a month ahead
Tours can be booked through their online ticketing or by
telephone.

Métro Line 14 to the Cour Saint-Emilion station

Note: Twice a year, the museum is open to free self-guided
tours and shows. This occurs during European Heritage
Days (usually the third weekend of September) and during
Le Festival du Merveilleux (December 26 to 31.)

Learn the Secrets of Paris'
Most Famous Cemetery

For some real Parisian chills, take a two hour, private guided tour of the infamous *Cimetière du Père Lachaise.* Opened in 1804, this is the city's largest graveyard and is now the eternal home of many famous artists, writers, politicians, musicians, and celebrities. Hear the stories of their lives (and their deaths) as you embark on a visit through it with a local expert. Historical details and fascinating anecdotes are what make this unusual walking tour so great. With more than seventy-thousand tombs in all, there's plenty to learn here.

babylontours.com
(Main site page) Click on Père Lachaise Cemetery Tour

Located at Boulevard Menilmontant & Rue de la Roquette
In the 11th arrondissement, Paris

Meeting point is just to the right of the Cemetery's main entrance

Calling from the US or Canada: (1) 702-481-8314
Calling from within Europe: (001) 702-481-8314

Email: babyloncitytours@gmail.com

Tours daily at 10am and 2pm
72 hour advance refund offered
Check availability on the calendar posted on the website above

Métro Line 2 to the Philippe Auguste station

Feel Spooked at the Famous Deyrolle Taxidermy Shop

A taxidermied animal is a strange thing to begin with, and to be literally surrounded by them is freakish to say the least. The French are well-known for their taxidermy and since 1831, Deyrolle's has been the premiere place to see and buy it. After a terrible fire a few years back, this famous shop is now up and running again. From bears to baby chicks, they seem to truly have it all. The shop has been featured in several films and might seem somehow familiar to you. Note: animal lovers will either love this or hate this.

deyrolle.com

Located at 46 Rue de Bac
In the 7th arrondissement, Paris

Intl. calling: (011) 33 1 42 22 30 07
Local calling: 01 42 22 30 07

Email: thomas.block@deyrolle.fr

Open Mondays 10am to 1pm / 2pm to 7pm
Open Tuesday through Saturday from 10am to 7pm
Closed Sundays and major holidays

Climb to the Dome of
Basilique du Sacré-Cœur

Some thrills come with challenging yourself. A climb to the dome of this basilica is one of them. Being atop the steep hill of Montmartre, its tower is one of the highest points in Paris. This means sweeping, unforgettable views but the way up there is daunting. If you feel up to a physical *and* mental challenge, go for it. You will be rewarded by the experience.

Access to the dome can be found outside the basilica to the left. You will have to fight any claustrophobia you might have as you climb the three-hundred steps. There is no elevator so this is the only way up *and* down. To fight off any panic, we recommend counting the steps so that you'll feel somewhat confident in knowing how far you have to go. Buy the very-affordable entry ticket on site.

sacre-coeur-montmartre.com

Located at 35 Rue de Chelvalier de la Barre
In the 18th arrondissement, Paris (Montmartre hill)

Intl. calling: (011) 33 1 53 41 89 00
Local calling: 01 53 41 89 00
Email contact available directly through their website

From May through September:
Dome access is open daily from 8:30am to 8pm

From April through October:
Dome access is open daily from 9am to 5pm

The hours above are subject to change and can vary according to the weather

Freak Out at Paris'
Strange Wax Museum

Paris' wax museum, *Le Musée Grévin,* is one of the oldest and most respected in Europe and a favorite among young Parisians. Not often visited by tourists, this place is much more than just wax figures, although there are hundreds of those to be seen. Special visual effects and other surprises that we can't tell you about definitely make this museum unique. There's a ton of creepy stuff too, especially in the French history wing. Torture, murder, plague, executions, and unfathomable medical practices are all on realistic display. They even have the actual bathtub and knife used in the assassination of Jean-Paul Marat in 1793. Bizarre!

This place is a bit pricey for an *open date* ticket so try to select a specific date from their online calendar and enjoy a substantial discount.

grevin-paris.com/en

Located at 10 Boulevard Montmartre
In the 9th arrondissement, Paris

Note: This street is not in the Montmartre neighborhood; it's in the Opéra area, not far from the Galleries Lafayette department store.

Intl. calling: (011) 33 1 47 70 85 05
Local calling: 01 47 70 85 05
Email contact available directly through their website

Open daily from 10am to 5pm (last entry)
Open Saturdays from 9:30am to 6pm (last entry)
Shorter hours on Christmas and New Year's Day

Métro Line 8 or 9 to the Grands Boulevards station

Go Underground to the Ossuary of the Catacombs

If you love the idea of going underground and walking through seemingly endless tunnels heaped with the bones of six-million people, then this is the sight for you. Just know that once inside, you'll have no choice but to continue through to the exit which is about an hour later because there are no exit points along the ossuary. Not even *emergency exits*. Make sure you're up to the task before committing yourself because you'll need to be in descent shape. It's claustrophobic and chilly, even in summer, and there's no bathroom, no bag check, and you'll need to climb a hundred and twelve steps of a spiral staircase in order to exit. Somehow this remains (no pun intended) one of Paris' most popular sights.

Not allowed:
People with accessibility issues, nervous conditions, in poor health, or pregnant/ Animals/ Children under age four

catacombes.paris.fr/en

Located at 1 Avenue du Colonel Henri Rol-Tanguy
Near Place Denfert-Rochereau
In the 14th arrondissement

Intl. calling: (011) 33 1 44 59 58 31
Local calling: 01 44 59 58 31 **or** 01 43 22 47 63
Email contact available directly through their website

Open Tuesday through Sunday from 10am to 7:30pm
The catacombs sometimes close earlier from October to March so call ahead
Closed Mondays/ Closed New Year's Day, May 1st, and Christmas Day

Part 8

Be a Child Again
❖ Places and activities to share with your kids ❖

If you're traveling to Paris with children then you should consider trying several of the fun activities in this very special chapter. Not only will your kids have fun doing them, they will make memories that will last forever.

How do you know your child can't bake macarons *if they've never tried?*

Try a Parent-Child Lesson in French Macaron Making

At Patisserie MiniMe, kids become a pastry chef! Mom and Dad can join the fun too if they want, making this a family experience you've probably never had before. You'll learn how to make perfect, delicate *macarons* and will even get to decorate them in fun and creative ways. The small group class is two hours long and you get to take your goodies with you in a special box. How difficult can it be?

minime-paris.com/macarons

"Chapellerie/Patisserie MiniMe"
Located at 75 Boulevard e Sébastopol (2nd floor)
In the 2nd arrondissement, Paris

Intl. calling: (011) 33 1 40 15 96 84
Local calling: 01 40 15 96 84

Email contact available directly through their website

Classes are held daily
Closed on major holidays

Check availability on the calendar posted on the website above
A 24 hour cancellation refund is offered

Visit the Animals
at Le Ménagerie

Twelve-hundred animals await you and your kids right in the city center. The zoo at Paris' botanical gardens, *Jardin des Plantes,* was opened in 1794 making it one of the world's first zoos. It's called *Le Ménagerie* and is, of course, a favorite of young Parisians. This haven of more than two-hundred species includes some that are endangered. As a research, conservation, and breeding center, these animals could not be in a better place.

There are red pandas, snow leopards, orangutans, bustards, giant tortoises, and white-naped cranes to name just a few. *Le Ménagerie* focuses on small to medium mammals and reptiles because they simply don't have the space for larger beasts like elephants. Even so, it's a wonderful place and will delight both young and old alike.

While you're there, take a ride on the *Dodo Manège* carousel which features only extinct animals. It's a fun learning tool that makes its point.

Le Ménagerie du Jardin des Plantes:

mnhn.fr/en/visit/lieux/menagerie-zoo-jardin-plantes
(A long but necessary URL)

Located at 57 Rue Cuvier
In the 5th arrondissement, Paris

Intl. calling: (011) 33 1 40 79 56 01
Local calling: 01 40 79 56 01

Email: valhuber@mnhn.fr

Open daily from 9am to 4:45pm (entry times)

Métro Line 7 or 10 to the Jussieu station

Ride in the World's Largest Helium Balloon

Ascend over Paris with your loved ones in a gondola hitched to the world's largest helium balloon. This gentle ride is a silent one as it rises (tethered) to a height of five-hundred feet. The views are breathtaking and there's just something cool about floating up in a helium balloon, a childhood dream if we've ever heard one. Plus, if you've always wanted to try a *hot* air balloon but are too afraid or on too tight of a budget, this is your ride.

The thrilling ten minute experience is offered on fair weather days from 9am until around sunset *as long as the winds above the city cooperate.* This can cause an abrupt cancellation but they do try to warn visitors by posting a live condition update on their website (below.) The management also encourages potential riders to **definitely call before heading over** in order to avoid any unnecessary disappointment.

Take the RER Train (Line C) from any of the Métro stations along the Seine's left bank going toward *Versailles Rive Gauche* **or** *St-Quentin-en Yveline* and disembark at the "Boulevard Victor-Pont" station. Or simply take a car service to the Parc André Citroën.

You'll see the ticket office near the launch area. When it's time to board, you'll step into the gondola of the balloon with up to thirty other people. For safety, there is always a trained balloon pilot on board. Go in the morning when it's less crowded.

ballondeparis.com

(continued)

Le Ballon de Paris Generali is
Located in the Parc André Citroën
In the 15th arrondissement, Paris

Intl. calling: (011) 33 1 44 26 20 00
Local calling: 01 44 26 20 00

Email: aeroparis@aerophile.com

Open daily from 9am to around sunset time
 -Atmospheric conditions permitting!
Closed on some major holidays

Enjoy a Family-Style
Scavenger Hunt in Montmartre

If you want to do something entertaining (and educational) with your kids but don't want to be pinned down to a certain date and time, choose this very flexible experience. All you do is grab this nifty, digitally pre-packaged scavenger hunt and follow its well thought-out game guide. Everything you need will be on your smart phone, and there's only one price for the whole gang, up to six people, at any age range. Before you know it, your loved ones will be peeking around *Sacré-Cœur* and running through the charming village of Montmartre. Solve riddles, identify landmarks and find clues as you compete, or work together, to discover things about your surroundings. There are about twenty challenges included. Since there's no human guide, you go when *you* want to, hopefully when the weather is cooperating. So fun!

touristscavengerhunt.com

The starting point is located at Place d'Anvers
(next to Métro station)
In the 9th arrondissement, Paris

Customer Service in the US: (514) 949-5201

Email: info@touristscavengerhunt.com

Métro Line 2 to the Anvers Station

Create an Original Perfume with Your Kids

Bond with your prince or princess while creating an original scent for each of you! Creating a unique fragrance with a French perfume expert is loads of fun and very educational. Spend two hours exploring the scents that you truly love and find out what affects the top and bottom notes... you'll both leave with your own bottle containing a never-before-heard-of *parfum* and will learn tons in the process. In addition, they will keep the exact formulas on file so that either fragrance can be reordered online. The lovely specialists at either *Le Studio des Parfum* or at *Atelier de Création de Parfum Candora* will make sure that you and your loved ones have a great time. Both studios are conveniently located on the Right Bank.

Check availability on the calendars posted on the websites below

Le Studio des Parfums:
studiodesparfums-paris.fr

Located at 23 Rue du Bourg Tibourg
In the 4th arrondissement, Paris

Intl. calling: (011) 33 1 40 29 90 84
Local calling: 01 40 29 90 84

Email: info@sdp-paris.**com**

Open Monday through Saturday from 11am to 7pm
Closed Sundays and major holidays

(continued)

Atelier de Création de Parfum Candora:
candora-fragrance.com

Located at 1 Rue du Pont Louis-Philippe
In the 4th arrondissement, Paris

Intl. calling: (011) 33 1 43 48 76 05
Local calling: 01 43 48 76 05

Email: contact@candora.fr

Open Monday through Saturday from 2pm to 7pm
Closed Sundays and major holidays

Race Toy Boats in the Pond
of Jardin des Tuileries

The beautiful Tuileries Gardens offers a beloved pastime of young Parisians. Since the turn of the last century, children have been using rods to navigate colorful wooden toy boats known as *petits voiliers* in a pond near the Louvre. Now antique, these exact same boats are still being rented out so that the tradition may continue. Relax on a nearby chair and watch while your children have fun the old fashioned way.

No official website

The toy boat rental cart is located next to the basin that's smack dab in the center of Jardin des Tuileries
In the 1st arrondissement, Paris

Rental cart is open from 11am to 3pm (in fair weather)
No limit of play hours if you have your own boat

Note: This fun diversion is also offered in the pond at the Luxembourg Gardens.

Do Some Serious Animal Watching at Parc Zoologique

The Paris Zoological Park has continued to get better and better since its historic opening in 1934. This is due in part to a €200 million renovation. The locals call it by many names: *Parc Zoologique de Paris*, *Bois de Vincennes Zoological Park*, and most commonly the *Vincennes Zoo.* It's all the same place though and unlike *Le Ménagerie* on the Left Bank, this one is huge. It has five "biozones," each with the appropriate animals enjoying the habitat it prefers. There are white rhinos, zebras, giraffes, lions, otters, and even manatees! It's world class. And if you get hungry you can head to one of its restaurants or enjoy your own spread at their picnic area.

parczoologiquedeparis.fr/en

Located on Avenue Daumesnil
In the 12th arrondissement, Paris

Intl. calling: (011) 33 8 11 22 41 22
Local calling: 08 11 22 41 22

Email contact available directly through their website

April, and also September through October
Open Monday through Friday from 9:30am to 5pm (entry time)
Open Saturdays & Sundays from 9:30am to 6:30pm (entry time)

June through August:
Open daily from 9:30am to 7:30pm (entry time)
Open later on Thursdays, **until 9pm (entry time)**

(continued)

<u>November through March</u>
Open daily (except Tuesdays) from 10am to 4pm (entry time)
Closed Tuesdays
Closed on major holidays so check their website for details

Métro Line 8 to the Porte Dorée station

Learn About Wizards
at the Museum of Magic

There's a magical museum right in the *Marais* that will make all of your little wizards very excited. The *Musée de la Magie* features magic wands, illusionist's props, divination trunks, spirit objects and all manner of magicians' paraphernalia. A visit there is always special for children but adults who are interested in the art and history of illusion will also have a wonderful time. There's even a fabulous magic show offered up every half hour!

museedelamagie.com

Located at 11 Rue Saint-Paul
In the 4th arrondissement, Paris

Intl. calling: (011) 33 1 42 72 13 26
Local calling: 01 42 72 13 26

Email: contact@museedelamagie.com

Open Wednesdays, Saturdays, & Sundays only from 2pm to 7pm

Ride through Paris
on Electric Scooters

Zipping through the streets of Paris on a seated or standing electric scooter (not the Moped type) is now *the* way to enjoy Paris. Whether you have a small tribe or a big one, rent your scooters from Rent&Go and become the hero of your family. They are easy to use and take all the legwork out of getting around this sprawling city. It's just so much fun!

rentngo.fr

<u>Shops located at:</u>

101 Avenue de la Bourdonnais
In the 7th arrondissement, Paris
or
19 Quai des Grands Augustins
In the 6th arrondissement, Paris

Intl. calling: (011) 33 6 32 97 33 11
Local calling: 06 32 97 33 11

Email contact available directly through their website

Open daily from 10:30am to 8pm
Closed on some major holidays

For a seamless rental, reserve your scooters ahead online

Have a Joyous Time at Paris' Own Amusement Park

Yes, there really is an amusement park right in Paris and your kids will love it. *Jardin d'Acclimatation* has fountains to splash in, play areas to run in, boats to travel in, workshops to take part in, coasters to thrill in, swing rides enjoy, farm animals to pet, and exotic birds to visit. Since 1931, this happy place west of the city center has delighted young locals and your kids should experience it too. This lush park even has an archery range, a mini golf course, a little train, a puppet show, a house of mirrors, and a children's science museum. Beat the queue by buying an e-ticket on their website.

jardindacclimatation.fr/en

Located in the Bois de Boulogne, Carrefour des Sablons
In the 16th arrondissement, Paris

Intl. calling: (011) 33 1 40 67 90 85
Local calling: 01 40 67 90 85

Email contact available directly through their website

Open Monday through Friday from 10am to 6pm (entry time)
Open Saturdays & Sundays and public holidays from 10am to 7pm (entry time)
Open year round

Métro Line 1 to the Les Sablons station

Note: Kids must be at least 31 inches tall to go on the rides. There are many other things to do in the Jardin besides the rides!

From the authors:

Thank you for reading *Bored in Paris*. We hope it gave you new insight and lots of inspiration to have fun experiences in the City of Lights. If you enjoyed it, please take a moment to leave a short customer review on Amazon so that your rating will count for us. Even a few sentences would be greatly appreciated.

Our blog is easily accessible and offers additional information to travelers. We also field any and all questions, comments, advice, and suggestions there: **cluedintravelbooks.com**

Thank you so much for your support. Check out all our *Bored In* travel books, exclusively on amazon.com.

Bored in Rome

Bored in Florence

Bored in Paris

Bored in Barcelona

Bored in London

Bored in Edinburgh

Bored in New York

Bored in San Francisco

Bored in Miami

bored in Paris

Index:

Part I - Try a Group Experience

Join a Super Fun Pub Crawl through the Latin Quarter p.3
See a French Film with English Subtitles p.4
Be Part of an Interactive Food Crawl in the Marais p.5
Join Parisians in a Serene Yoga Class p.6
Savor a Pop Up Dinner in a Chef's Own Flat p.7
Join a Crêpe-Making Luncheon on the Left Bank p.8
Rollerblade at Night with Thousands of Enthusiasts p.9
Explore Monet's Gardens with a Group Visit to Giverny p.11

Part II - Connect with Nature

Go Horseback Riding in the Bois de Boulogne p.15
Jog along an Abandoned Elevated Railway Line p.16
Try a Full Day Bike Tour of Versailles p.17
Tour the Monuments on an Electric Scooter p.18
Have a Picnic in the City's Loveliest Green Space p.19
Splash in a Floating Swimming Pool on the Seine p.20
Rent a City Bike during Sunset p.21
Visit the Eco-Friendly Village Nature de Paris p.23

Part III - Learn Something New

Indulge in a Wine Tasting Workshop p.27
Try a Lesson in French Croissant-Making p.28
Take a Special Night Tour of Le Musée du Louvre p.29
Find Your Inner Julia at Le Cordon Bleu p.30
Create an Original Fragrance at a French Perfumery p.31
Learn to Make Classic French Desserts p.33
Take a Workshop of Parisian Hat-Making p.35
Enjoy Cheese & Wine Pairings in a 17th Century Cellar p.36

Part IV - Search for Something

Shop the Paris Flea Market with a Connoisseur p.39
Take a Private Shopping Trip with a Parisian Stylist p.40
Weigh in on Fashion at the Kilo Shop p.41
Visit a Shop that's Bursting with Upcycled Goods p.42
See the Top Fashion Boutiques of the Golden Triangle p.43
Peruse through France's Oldest Flea Market p.44
Go Antiquing on the Left Bank p.46
Visit the Most Beautiful Wine Store in Paris p.47

Part V - Have an Engrossing Individual Experience

Surrender to a Half-Day French Spa Experience p.51
Learn Salsa Dancing the French Way p.52
Experience the "Pure Chocolate" Walking Tour p.53
Admire Art in a Preserved 19th Century Mansion p.54
Critique Avant-Garde Photography at Jeu de Paume p.55
Benefit from a One-on-One Styling Experience p.56
Find Your New Haircut in a Paris Salon p.57
Challenge Yourself in a Paris Running Event p.58
Become the Art with a Permanent Souvenir p.60

Part VI - Make Memories

Taste Wines with an Expert p.63
Be Spellbound by Immersive Digital Art p.64
Indulge at a Parisian Jazz Club p.65
Dine in Absolute Darkness at Dans le Noir Restaurant p.66
Order up a Romantic, Professionally-Catered Picnic p.67
Be Tempted by Ubiquitous Apple at Restaurant Pomze p.68
Have a Professional Photo Shoot around Town p.69
Dine Inside the Oldest Building in Paris p.70
Chill Out at the Frozen Ice Kube Bar p.71
Have Dinner on the Eiffel Tower p.72
Take a Champagne Cruise on the River Seine p.73
Attempt to Find the Entrance of a Speakeasy p.75
Attend a Performance at the Magnificent Palais Garnier p.76

Part VII - Local Thrills and Chills

Take a Spectacular Hot Air Balloon over Fontainebleau p.79
Ride on Creepy Carnival Attractions from the 1800's p.80
Learn the Secrets of Paris' Most Famous Cemetery p.82
Feel Spooked at the Famous Deyrolle Taxidermy Shop p.83
Climb to the Dome of Basilique du Sacré-Cœur p.84
Freak Out at Paris' Strange Wax Museum p.85
Go Underground to the Ossuary of the Catacombs p.87

Part VIII - Be a Child Again

Try a Parent-Child Lesson in French Macaron Making p.91
Visit the Animals at Le Ménagerie p.92
Ride in the World's Largest Helium Balloon p.93
Enjoy a Family-Style Scavenger Hunt in Montmartre p.95
Create an Original Perfume with Your Kids p.96
Race Toy Boats in the Pond of Jardin des Tuileries p.98
Do Some Serious Animal Watching at Parc Zoologique p.99
Learn About Wizards at the Museum of Magic p.101
Ride through Paris on Electric Scooters p.102
Have a Joyous Time at Paris' Own Amusement Park p.103

For more information on Paris,
visit our Clued In/Bored In website and blog at
cluedintravelbooks.com

Disclaimer:

Every effort has been made for accuracy. The authors, publishers, and webmasters take no responsibility for consequences or mishaps while using this website, nor are they responsible for any difficulties, inconveniences, injuries, illness, medical mishaps, or other physical issues related to the information and suggestions provided in this website. The information contained in this website is for diversionary purposes only. Any mentions in this website do not represent an endorsement of any group or company or their practices, methods, or any mishaps that may occur when hired or participated in.

While we endeavor to have all content up to date and correct, we make no representations, guarantees, or warranties of any kind, express or implied, about the completeness, accuracy, reliability, suitability or availability with respect to the book or its information, products, services, companies, or related graphics contained within, for any purpose. Any reliance you place on such information is therefore strictly at your own risk. In no event will we be liable for any loss or damage including without limitation, indirect or consequential loss or damage, or any loss or damage whatsoever arising from loss of data, monies, or profits, arising out of, or in connection with, the use of this book.

Throughout this book are websites which are not under the control of *Bored In Travel Books* or *Clued In Travel Books* or the authors, associates, or publishers thereof. We have no control over the nature, content, appropriateness, and availability of the websites, tours, shops, or experiences mentioned. The inclusion of any web-links mentioned should not imply a recommendation of them, nor endorse the views expressed within them. The authors, associates and publishers of this book take no responsibility for, and will not be liable for, the web-links or associated websites being temporarily unavailable due to technical issues beyond our control, or any mishaps occurring from such issues.

All designations used by companies to distinguish their products are often claimed as trademarks. All brand names and product names used in this book are trade names, service marks, trademarks, and registered trademarks of their respective owners. The authors, publishers, and the book are not at all associated with any product, vendor, shop, tour, or companies mentioned in this book. None of the companies referenced within the book have endorsed or supported it in any way.

my notes